# GOD & ME & MY MODEL T AND OTHER GOOD STORIES

## IT CAME UPON A MIDNIGHT CLEAR

I pray that this book of short stories
can give you an assurance that God
has blessings in store for your life.
If He can accept even me, there is hope
for everyone!    God bless you.

Matt. 22: 37-40

# Bill Scott

*Bill Scott*

ISBN 978-1-63874-491-7 (paperback)
ISBN 978-1-63874-492-4 (digital)

Christian Faith Publishing, Inc.
832 Park Avenue
Meadville, PA 16335
www.christianfaithpublishing.com

Printed in the United States of America

# GOD AND ME AND MY MODEL T

# GOD AND ME AND MY MODEL T

---

AT A RECENT CHURCH renewal event, the pastor was making a point about the various words the Ancient Greeks used that we have generically translated into one word: *love*. After a lengthy explanation, the speaker commented that we cannot love an inanimate object. Love is reciprocal; you can't love something that can't love you back. I leaned over to my wife and whispered, "I love my Model T."

The object of my affection is a 1926 Model T Ford roadster. My father-in-law bought it for me at an auction sale. He brought it to me as a pile of loose parts hauled in on a flatbed trailer. It was what a car nut would call a "basket case." I had a frame, two axles with the springs and spindles separated from them, a derelict engine and transmission, and a stack of sheet metal parts in various stages of abuse, rust, and dents. Accompanying this eclectic collection were several fifty-five-gallon drums full of loose parts.

It was obvious that this mix of parts that had once been an automobile was in a bad state of neglect. Someone in the past had cast it aside as worthless when another person saw value in that beat-up and damaged old relic. In an effort to save it from the scrap heap, that person had torn the car apart and started to restore it to its original dignity. As with many things in life, the salvation became too much effort, and that wonderful machine from the past was again rejected. This was what was purchased by my father-in-law. I had the opportunity to make something once considered to be worthless into a wonderful dream machine!

*****

In our personal lives, we can get so worn down and beat up that we feel we are worthless and only destined for the scrap heap. Jesus paid the price to buy us from the "scrap agent." (We all know who that is!) Now the restoration begins.

*****

I lovingly rebuilt the engine, transmission, suspension, and the rear-end gear set. I repaired any damaged components or replaced them with new ones. If the parts needed weren't available, I made my own. Usually the replacement was better than the original. The dents and damage that gave evidence to living a hard life were repaired and massaged into an object that could bring pleasure and joy to our family and to many others.

\*\*\*\*\*

God has done no less with our lives. He has repaired our poorly functioning inner workings and changed our status from a derelict social reject into something to be admired and appreciated.

\*\*\*\*\*

Some parts of my car are still dented, and there is paint that is less than perfect. These areas are that way so I can remember that it will never be perfect, just as I am not perfect. There is always work to do to improve this vehicle I am riding around in. God is not done with me either. My car does not exactly match the blueprint that Ford drew up nearly one hundred years ago. I have departed from the original design as needed to make my vintage car more adapted to its current use.

God has a plan for each of our lives: "I knew you before you were formed within your mother's womb; before you were born I had a plan for you" (Jeremiah 1:5). My life does not match the original plan that God had for me either. I was cruising down the wrong road far too long. But He did not give up on me, and when I became available, He bought me and paid a price with Jesus's life. When He got me from the scrap heap, He used what He had and modified His original plan to fit the current use.

*****

My car has nonstandard, twelve-volt, sealed-beam headlights so I can see down the road where God is sending me. I have modern-style directional lights so other people can identify where I am going. And hopefully they won't run into me and knock me off course. The brakes on my car have been upgraded so that when I recognize dangers ahead, I can stop before it is too late.

*****

I love my Model T. My little car has become a symbolic metaphor of our cast-off lives that have been restored and renewed to live a fascinating new lifestyle. It is a reminder of the salvation and grace that God has brought to all of us.

If your life seems like a wreck that is destined for the scrap heap, just remember that *God is searching for another project to restore.* If you turn your life over to Him, the Master Craftsman will take any basket case, no matter how badly beat up. He will make you into something that is lovely and useful and will draw admiration from all. Open up your heart and let Jesus in, then fasten your seat belt and hang on; you are about to take the most exciting ride you could ever imagine!

# THE KID WHO WAS TOO SMALL TO BE AN ATHLETE

# THE KID WHO WAS TOO SMALL TO BE AN ATHLETE

HE GREW UP IN Kewanee, Illinois—a town of about fourteen thousand in population on the northwestern side of the state. Bill Scott was smaller than the other boys his age but had a tightly wound spring inside that always begged for adventure.

He was a boy who loved sports, but his obvious size limitations (five feet, one-half inch, one hundred pounds) eliminated him from high school participation in the popular sports even if he had good balance and reflexes like a cat. Schools in the '50s hadn't yet accepted wrestling, where size and weight divisions were essential to make a full team. He went for track during his sophomore year and practiced hard. His short legs made the dash events a poor option. But his endurance could qualify him for the mile or cross-country team. When the lineup was posted, his name was not listed among the team members even though slower distance runners were on the roster. Bill went in and asked the coach why he was left off the team and many of the slower runners were on.

The coach's reply was, "Track is not really a sport. It is actually an in-between season that I use to keep my athletes in shape for football. You are too small. You will never be an athlete. You might as well learn to accept that."

He was crushed by the coach's insensitive attitude.

Little Bill went to the locker room, changed into street clothes, went outside, and climbed on his motorcycle, nursing a bad mood. In his anger, he pulled his Harley dirt bike onto the quarter-mile track and proceeded to turn it loose, enjoying the pleasure of broadsliding nasty grooves with knobby tires into the smooth, nicely groomed cinder track. He later had to spend detention time raking the track into shape for the balance of the season, angry that the coach was benefiting from his efforts.

That experience with the coach turned Bill off to popular sports—indeed, most extracurricular activities. He directed his attention to motorcycle racing where he was a standout participant. The size factor meant less weight and extra horsepower to go faster, and a fine sense of coordination and reflexes illustrated athletic capabilities the coach hadn't recognized.

In 1958, Bill made the big move. He decided to try his luck at professional racing events. After saving every penny he could from a job as an auto mechanic, he bought a new Harley-Davidson 750 cc racing machine and acquired an American Motorcycle Association professional competition license.

As a novice rider, it was limited as to the events where one can participate.

Nevertheless, during the first year, he won the Novice Class at Laconia, New Hampshire, the Novice Class at Marlboro, Maryland, and placed third at Peoria, Illinois—all on national championship tracks.

On September 21, 1958, the season wrap-up in Fort Worth, Texas, was a road race on a very fast airport course (Bill was already a high-point novice in the nation). He set a track record in the heat race and earned the right to start on the pole for the final, lined up alongside some very important names in the racing world. The flag dropped, and he shot into the lead for two laps when a local Texan came into a corner too hard, trying to pass on the inside. The local fellow fell down and, sliding sideways, took Bill out, throwing him over the "high side." (In cycle racing, this is when you are leaning into a corner and the bike is lifted to slingshot you off the apex of the turn.)

The track officials later stated they figured he slid something around three hundred fifty to four hundred feet, resulting in skid marks in seven directions on the helmet and a leather racing suit that looked like shredded suede. The ambulance crew thought they were picking up a corpse. The human body just can't take that kind of abuse and survive! At the hospital, it was discovered that he had a concussion, a badly crushed right shoulder, along with other miscellaneous broken bones, and abrasions over the entire body. An orthopedic surgeon in Peoria told him that he would lose approximately 20 percent of the rotation in the right arm even after extensive surgery.

This was quite a setback because Bill had his sights set on competing at Daytona Beach the next March for the biggest prize in motorcycling. He had qualified to move up to the AMA Amateur Class—the equivalent to today's Nationwide Class in NASCAR. In December, the doctors released him to try some rehab exercises. His own personal workout far exceeded what the doctors recommended. By March, he had recovered all lost arm movement and was doing fifty pushups twice a day.

They went to Daytona with a motorcycle; that was no insignificant accomplishment itself. Lacking financial wealth and having no sponsors, the race team consisted of a brother, a cousin, and a friend. The oldest member of the team was twenty. What they lacked in finances and technical accessibility was more than made up for with enthusiasm. They rebuilt the machine that had been crashed at Fort Worth and carefully hand-fitted every part; nothing was too small to escape meticulous attention. The transmission gears were lapped so they would mesh to perfection; they blueprinted every part to work perfectly. The resultant machine was not long on the greatest technology, but it was very smooth and durable and race-ready.

It was intimidating to appear at Daytona with a race team that consisted of four teenagers to do battle with the best factory teams from around the world. There were the Japanese teams with engineers using radar guns to clock riders during practice, then doing calculations on their abacus and writing notes that only they could read.

They saw the European factory team riders who were treated like thoroughbred race horses; they saw mind-boggling racing machines with exotic items that were not affordable even in their wildest dreams.

After time trials down the beach, the kids from Kewanee made their presence known with the third fastest time. Saturday morning of race day brought over one hundred anxious racers lined up on the beach for the starting gun (a smoky cannon shot). One hour and four minutes later, the race was over, and the home-brewed race bike had put over a four-mile lead (two minutes, thirty-nine seconds) over everyone else. They had just won one of the biggest races in the world. Four teenagers from a little town in western Illinois with a rider who "will never be an athlete" because he was "too small."

When Bill returned home, he was the local folk hero for a time, but he still had something that had to be done. He took the trophy from Daytona to the high school and went into the coach's office to remind him of the time he had told the youngster he would never be an athlete. He had to show the coach the trophy from Daytona Beach, one of the most coveted championship icons a motorsports athlete could ever wish to acquire. There were world-class athletes clamoring to have such a memory in their showcase!

Bill's son is now a high school football and wrestling coach.

He has strict instructions from his father that he shall never treat a student in such a manner as that coach treated him. Following his dad's orders, Bill's son, Greg Scott, has coached many champions in wrestling as well as three football players who have made it to the NFL. Every boy is an athlete if he has desire, heart, and the attitude to work for the coveted gold ring.

Now you know the rest of the story.

Laconia N.H. 1959

Daytona 2010
Vintage Racing on 55 yr. old Bike (Restored)
Rider is 71 Yrs Old!
Finished 2nd in competition against riders 1/2 that age

"When you have won at Daytona, nothing else in your resume matters!
(Dale Earnhart, Sr.)

Daytona 1959
Other Rider is being lapped.
#59 was 2min 39 sec. ahead of 2nd place.

BILL SCOTT

Daytona 1959

Daytona 1959

Lacona N.H.

Illustrations by grandson, Ryan Scott

# IT CAME UPON A MIDNIGHT CLEAR

# IT CAME UPON A MIDNIGHT CLEAR

---

## A Good Children's Story

IT WAS A FALL afternoon when José and Maria were traveling down Interstate 80, headed to Chicago. They were required to report to immigration to update José's work visa.

His employment as a carpenter had wound down when the fall weather had closed in on the construction season.

This seemed like an ideal occasion for José to take some time off and head for the government offices for the registry. The weather had turned cold and blustery with a strong west wind that buffeted their truck on the highway.

Their pickup truck had been outfitted for just such a special journey. Since José was a skilled carpenter, he had prepared a comfortable sleeping area in his compact travel trailer. He also had carefully allowed accessible cubbyholes for his prized collection of the special tools of his trade.

Maria, being in the third trimester of her pregnancy, was trying her best to remain comfortable. José reminded her of the visit by the angel Gabriel.

He reminded his wife how the angel had assured them that God would be with them wherever they were sent. Even though she implicitly trusted the Lord and had the deepest faith, it was a nervous feeling she felt deep within her being. She knew this baby was very special—the angel had announced that fact. Yet she was young and did not know what to expect, being so far from her family connections.

On their travel down the highway, Maria commented to José how she had been very frightened when the angel Gabriel had appeared to her. The angel was such an imposing image, huge and glowing with a strange light surrounding him. But when he spoke, his voice was so gentle and soothing, she knew there was nothing to fear. He assured her that God had noticed her purity and goodness. She was chosen to bring a new life to the earth—a life that would change the world forever. God had chosen Maria to become a blessing to all humanity!

Their truck had given them problems, and a stop at a garage in Iowa for a fuel pump had put them two days behind their expected schedule and greatly depleted their travel money. With extra drag from towing the camper and the windy weather, their gas mileage was not in the economy category. The gas gauge was showing a low level. José needed to find a short-term project that needed a carpenter.

He saw a small town exit at Morris, Illinois, and pulled off to seek someone who needed his talents. Experience had taught him that the police station was a place where they knew what was happening in the entire community.

"How is it going, Maria? Can you hold out a while longer?"

She commented, "My comfort is at a low level, but I am not in any big pain. You must do what you have to do. I know we need some money to continue."

Finding the local police station, José walked up to the information desk and asked if they knew of anyone who needed a skilled carpenter. The middle-aged lady at the desk was taken aback by José's eyes that expressed a deepness she had never seen in all her years in police work. Intuitively she knew she had someone she could trust.

"Sarge!" she yelled out to her command officer. "I have a fellow here who is short on gas money, and he claims to be a good carpenter."

The sergeant stepped up to the desk, wondering about the unusually enthusiastic calling of his desk clerk.

She stepped back a few steps and quietly said to her boss, "That door on the garage that the wind had whipped so hard that it won't close should be repaired for the security of our squad cars besides all the equipment in the garage."

"Naw, that is too big a job for just a handyman. That's going to take a whole new door. It's all twisted and sprung. The jamb is split, and the hinges are bent. That's too much work for just a quick fix."

"Just give him a try. If he can even get the door to close, it would be a big help."

Finally the sergeant relented. "So, you say you are a good carpenter?"

"Sí, very good!"

"We have a bit of a problem with an entry door that the wind has torn off the hinges. Can you at least get it to close in an afternoon?"

"Sí, I can fix 'em."

"If you can get it to close, I have fifty dollars in a cash fund to pay you for your efforts."

The sergeant took him to the back garage and showed the broken and sprung door to José, commenting, "We don't have any supplies on hand, so you're on your own."

"I believe I have all the supplies I need for this little project. Can my wife sit inside while I work? She is late in her pregnancy."

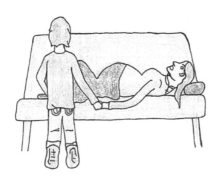

"Oh, sure. There is a couch in the vestibule. My clerk will make her comfortable."

Maria was helped into the warmth and comfort of the entryway, and immediately José went to work on the door, humming happily. An hour and a half later, José reported to the desk clerk that the project was finished and ready for inspection.

The clerk accompanied José back to the garage to see what he had accomplished in such a short time.

"*Wow!*" she exclaimed. "I can't believe you were able to even get that broken door to close, much less function as smoothly as this. It moves like a brand-new door."

"Hey, Sarge! You gotta see this!" she yelled into her collar-mounted radio.

He recognized the astonishment in her voice, so he was there quickly.

"Look at that door!" she stated in amazement.

The officer carefully checked the repairs. "I can't believe it!" he said. "That door was bent out of shape, the jamb was split, and the hinges were sprung. Now I can't even find a crack in the wood. The door swings smoothly and closes with perfection. I don't know how you did it!"

José just smiled with a sly little grin and his eyes looking upward.

"I was sure there was at least a three-hundred-dollar investment to get that door back to usable service. You did it in less than two hours, and it looks like a perfect repair. That fifty I promised you, I'm going to double. Deborah, get José here a hundred dollars out of the emergency facilities fund."

José and Maria got their tank filled with gasoline, then stopped at a drive-through for a quick lunch, and soon they were back on the road, headed to their appointment in Chicago. The wind and cold continued as they traveled on. However, the delay had brought birth pangs at ever-closer intervals. Finally José pulled off the expressway at Joliet, following the blue signs that indicated a hospital / trauma center was near.

Checking at the emergency entrance, they were questioned about insurance coverage.

"Do you have Medicaid?"

"No."

"Do you have insurance of any kind?"

"I don't have insurance coverage. This is a new experience to me," José replied.

She snobbishly stated, "With so many complications in the birthing process and lawsuits being what they are, we can't admit anyone who does not have insurance."

So it was back in the truck, and they continued.

"Well, Maria, we will just have to keep moving."

"But the labor pains are getting closer as the time ticks by," she said.

José replied, "Remember how the angel had promised that God would provide for our safety and well-being. We must trust His promises."

As they continued through town, José spotted a parking deck that would provide protection from the wind and rain. He hurriedly prepared the bed that he had so carefully built into their compact travel trailer. José helped Maria into the comfort of the travel bed where she rested easily. Within minutes, the time had come, and Maria proceeded to give birth to her baby boy.

Instantly the parking deck was awash with light; a heavenly glow filled every corner of the parking garage. Nearby, a police car was patrolling.

"Hey, Mac, what do ya think? The public calls us their guardians."

Mac replied, "Aren't we supposed to be the public shepherds?"

To that, O'Reilly commented, "What kind of shepherds are we when one considers the level of crime and criminal activity in our precinct? It seems like we are failures in the shepherd description."

Then they suddenly noticed the unusual glow in the downtown area. This was so unusual, following good police practice, it required investigation. As Mac and O'Reilly headed for the downtown, they radioed their shift commander to report the situation they had decided to chase down. Mac and O'Reilly headed toward the source of the glow when they noticed a light pillar in the sky similar to an advertising beam from a giant spotlight. But this light reached higher into the sky than any spotlight they had ever seen, and it focused directly on the downtown parking garage. In this case, the light was not created at the base; it seemed to be shining down directly from the sky. The squad cars converged at the parking garage to witness an area flooded with an eerie light that defied explanation.

The three policeman stepped out of their cars and instantly realized the wind and rain had suddenly stopped and a still calm had come upon the area.

"What the heck is happening?"

Then in the quiet after the storm, there was a sound of music distinctly filling the whole area. The music was not loud; it just surrounded them with a soft, symphonic sound that filled them right down to their bones.

As the police stood gazing into the sky, they realized the music had come directly from heaven above. They could clearly see the sky was filled with angels singing praises to God. O'Reilly was first to drop to his knees, cross himself, and worship the scene that was directly in front of them. Soon all three were on their knees. Their commander was flat on the ground, humbling himself in the prone position. They knew they were in the process of witnessing a heaven-sent miracle.

1 Corinthians 15:23

Christ was raised as the first of the harvest; then all who belong to christ will be raised when he comes back

Mac commented that the Scriptures had often told of Jesus returning to the earth to sort the good people from the evil. Intuitively they knew their eyes were seeing the opening of a new paradigm in world history.

Those policemen stayed at the scene for the whole evening. Time seemed to mean nothing in view of all their eyes were witnessing.

"Hey, Mac, do you want a ride home? Your shift has been over for several hours."

He replied, "You couldn't get me to leave this if you had a troop of armed soldiers."

Early the next morning, just as the sun was beginning to appear, the pillar of light was still clearly visible. Suddenly a Lincoln sedan pulled up to the garage. Three men climbed out of the car and introduced themselves as astronomers working at the University of Chicago. They had been closely studying the unusual conjunction of stars in the sky. When the pillar of light appeared, there was no question. They knew immediately what had happened, and they must go to the source of that light. The three professors bowed down in reverent esteem to the new infant.

The first professor reached into his wallet and presented José with a prepaid American Express Gold card.

"This will provide you with enough to give a good life for the boy until he is capable of reaching out on his own."

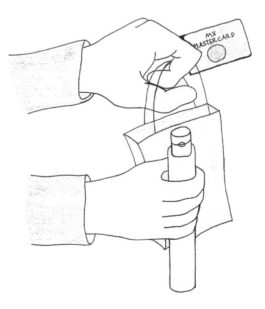

The second stepped forward and gave Maria a large bottle of a special-formula baby lotion that had been compounded in the university lab. It would be helpful to keep the child comfortable through his diaper period.

The third presented the parents with a very exquisite ointment intended to make the child smell and feel as good as any member of royalty.

The hardened policemen, who thought they had seen everything, stood in awe. They could not believe what they were witnessing. Deep down they knew this night's event would be a turning point in the history of the world.

These events had a great impact on José and Maria as they admired their new son.

Gabriel had told them to expect a lot of fanfare when the boy was born. The whole world had been in turmoil with crime and evil people dominating society. Their son was destined to change all that. The world had been waiting for over two thousand years, and now their small select group of people had witnessed a new era in world history.

God was reaching down from heaven and infusing blessings on all humanity!

# WHAT DOES EASTER MEAN?

# WHAT DOES EASTER MEAN?

EASTER MEANS SPRING, THE rebirth of life that has gone dormant all winter.

It is a reminder that our faith needs a rebirth.

Easter is a memorial to the death and the victory over death that our Lord Jesus Christ experienced so we could all know that God will call us to Him as our final reward.

We are reminded He suffered beating, humiliation, and a kangaroo court that condemned our Lord to death by a slow, painful lynching—nailed to a rough wooden cross.

Do we ever stop to consider the pain, the terror, the shock of this form of condemnation? When he was placed on the sturdy, wooden beams, His mind must have been filled with agony as the scene was taking shape.

The heavy hammers rose and fell forcing nails to crash through bone and flesh while His blood flooded to the surface.

The pain, oh, the pain, as the body system goes into shock!

The executioners then raised the cross to allow the sun and time to finish their chore.

Prior to Jesus, the Roman cross was a symbol of cruel execution by a brutal torture. The cross had about as much appeal as a hangman's noose! Since Jesus's death and victory over death, the cross has become a source of pride to Christians. It decorates churches and serves as jewelry identifying believers. The Roman symbol of shame has been juxtaposed to represent the greatest wonder God has ever brought to our planet!

Two convicts were also crucified at Jesus's side. They lashed out with curses and screams of agony to their tormentors.

One of the criminals turned to Jesus and asked Him to "remember me when you arrive in your kingdom" (Luke 23:42 NIV).

Jesus told him that "today you will join me in paradise." A last-minute acceptance of Jesus won that criminal a free ticket to eternity in paradise.

Then, turning and looking at His executioners, our Lord turned his eyes to heaven and, in a calm, apologetic voice, said, "Forgive them, Father; they don't know what they are doing" (Luke 23:34 NIV).

He was even willing to forgive the men who were putting him to death through the slow and painful torture of the cross! Jesus's death and resurrection is our assurance that the Lord offers forgiveness and a seat in paradise for eternity.

That is what Easter means!

But the grave could not contain our Lord, the Son of God!

Three days later, He arose from the tomb to take His place as our Savior, our access to heaven. He died that we might have life.

His life continues to this day in the dedication of his followers. The world has been changed by one man's feat of personal sacrifice.

An act to illustrate the saving grace of our Heavenly Father.

Jesus Christ was raised from the dead to give *us* life everlasting.

A life in eternity with God.

This is Easter!

# ABOUT THE AUTHOR

"God & Me & My Model T" And Other Good Stories

BILL SCOTT STARTED RACING a motorcycle at age fifteen; by eighteen, he turned to the professional circuit. He won championship races at Daytona Beach, Laconia, New Hampshire, and Marlboro, Maryland. He apprenticed four years at a Chevy dealership as a GM Certified Technician and four years at Caterpillar as a toolmaker.

Bill owned a Harley-Davidson dealership for seventeen years, preparing racing bikes that won several national championships, then sold it after nationwide financial crunch in 1984. He wrote the weekly newspaper column "Scotty Says" featuring motorcycle activities.

Bill returned to college to acquire a bachelor's degree in industrial technology and enhanced it with an MBA. He then became a maintenance superintendent at an edible oil refinery owned by Lipton.

Bill attended a two-year study at Bethel Bible Institute in Madison, Wisconsin, and taught adult Bible studies for nearly fifty years at the local Presbyterian Church. He now has a weekly email ministry involving a self-written commentary following the common lectionary; this outreach includes over four hundred recipients including over fifty pastors and goes worldwide.

Bill Scott has been married for fifty-nine years with three children, four grandchildren, and one great-granddaughter! His Model T hobby in retirement includes eight family Model Ts.

Bill has a well-equipped shop that has become the "go to" destination for Model T hobbyists within a one hundred mile circle.

CPSIA information can be obtained
at www.ICGtesting.com
Printed in the USA
BVHW090737271021
619746BV00004B/25